D1502279

WHAT'S THE BIG IDEA?

ALPHABET

Pamela J.P. Schroeder
Jean M. Donisch

ROURKE PUBLICATIONS, INC.
VERO BEACH, FL 32964

A book by Market Square Communications Incorporated.
A special thanks to out creative team, Sandy Robinson, Sandra Shekels and
Ann Garber of Market Square Communications Incorporated, for their creative
text and design contributions.

Consultants:
> Jeanette L. Handrich — M.A. in Elementary Education/Language Arts,
> third and fourth grade teacher/gifted and talented
> program, over 20 years teaching experience
> Karen M. Olsen — M.S. in Education, kindergarten teacher,
> over 20 years teaching experience
> Geri Pape — M.S. in Elementary Education, kindergarten teacher, over 30
> years teaching experience

Library of Congress Cataloging-in-Publication Data
Schroeder, Pamela J. P., 1969-
    Alphabet / Pamela J.P. Schroeder, Jean M. Donisch.
       p. cm. — (What's the big idea?)
    Summary: Labeled illustrations and rhyming text introduce
each letter of the alphabet. Includes related questions and
activities.
    ISBN 0-86625-576-1
    1. English language—Alphabet—Juvenile literature.
[1. Alphabet.] I. Donisch, Jean M., 1960-   . II. Title.
III. Series.
PE1155.S36   1996
[E]—dc20   95-26571
                                       CIP
                                       AC

Printed in the U.S.A.

TABLE OF CONTENTS

For more fun with ALPHABET ideas, look for this shape at the bottom of the page.

ABOUT THE ALPHABET

**Big ideas start out small
With just 26 letters —
The alphabet
That's all!**

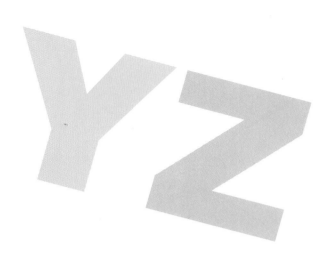

All you need
To spell any word
Is 26 letters,
Any word that you've heard!

Words are bigger than letters,
But not big enough.
Ideas need words in a sentence
To strut their stuff.

Mix words up, put them in a row —
Making a sentence is easy
Now that you know!

With letters, words and sentences,
You can make big ideas grow!

Aa

acorns

alligator

apple

bowl

airplane

apron

What do **a**nts eat for breakfast? Do they like butter or bread?
Would they rather have **a**pples and **a**corns instead?

6

bagels

Bb

buns

basket

banana

bread

butter

ant

bottle

balls

bell

buttons

What foods can you think of that start with A or B?

When ants eat bananas, do they like the peel,
Or are bagels and buns a better meal?

7

Cc

daisy

clown

caramel apple

cage

door

camel

cats

cotton candy

chain

In a **c**age at the **c**ir**c**us, you might see a big **c**at
Or a **c**lown with a **d**aisy stuck in his hat.

A **d**og could **d**rive a **c**ar around center ring,
Or you might see a **c**ow who's learned to sing!

Ee eagle

feathers

egg

goldfish

Eskimo

fox

fish

Ff

Eagles lay **e**ggs in nests high off the ground.
Foxes hide in the **g**rass and don't like to be found.

Earth

Gg

giraffe

glove

foot

grass

grasshopper

frog

What animals live where Eskimos live?

Frogs sit next to streams where fish swim and play.
Earth is a beautiful home. Let's keep it that way.

11

Hh

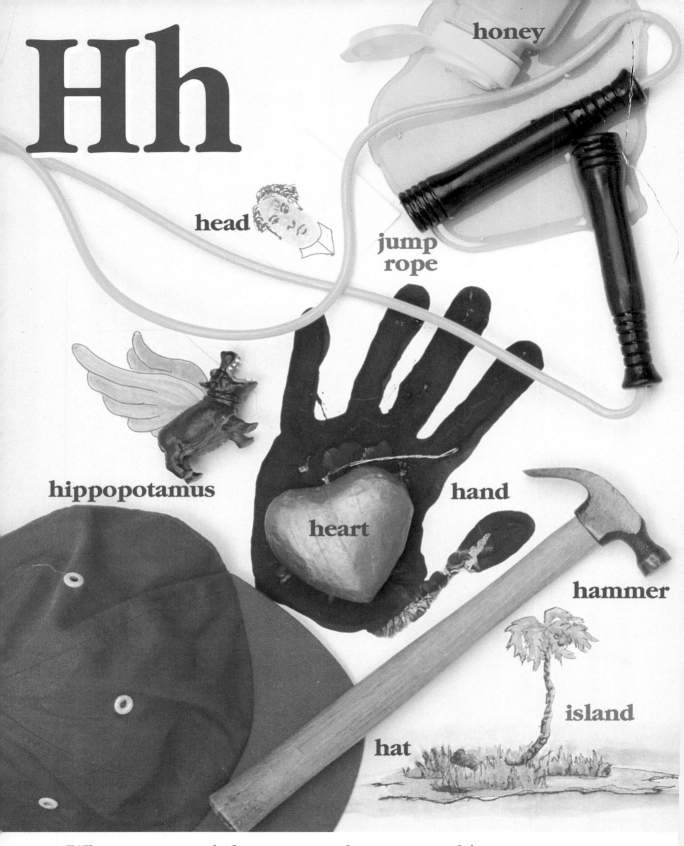

honey

head

jump rope

hippopotamus

heart

hand

hammer

island

hat

When you use **i**nk, you can draw crazy things —
Iguanas eating **i**ce cream, or a **h**ippopotamus with wings.

horn

jet

Jj

ice cream

iguana

jar

jelly

ink

Ii

Can you share a story about a time when you spilled something?

With your pen you can make an island float in honey,
Or a horn that squirts jelly — that would be funny!

13

Kk

letter

To: My Pen Pal
600 Happy St
Anytown NY 00000

lakes

lobster

lemon

lips

kiss

lizard

key

Would leopards and lions live on the same street?
Would a ladybug, lamb and lizard ever meet?

14

Ll

king

logs

leaf

kite

lion

leopard

ladybug

killer whale

lamb

Write a letter to someone special.

Where could you find a big **k**iller whale?
Would a **k**ing get a **l**etter you sent in the mail?

monkey

nail

magnet

needle

moccasin

mask

noodles

nose

nine

mouth

Mm

necklace

Monkeys don't wear moccasins because they don't fit.
They might put on a necklace to dress up a bit.

Nn

net

nests

marbles

mouse

nuts

moon

napkins

What do you see when you look in a mirror?

A **mouse** could eat the **moon** if it were made of cheese,
Then wipe its **mouth** on a **napkin**, as nice as you please.

17

Oo

owl

pig

orange

onion

olive

pear

octopus

octagon

panda

penguin

If you were a **p**irate, what would be on your ship?
Some **p**eanuts to snack on, some **o**range juice to sip —

18

peanuts

P p

polar bear

oval

paddles

puzzle

parrot

pirate

Make up a story about an octopus and a penguin.

A **p**enguin or a **p**anda for company,
And some **p**addles to row across the wide open sea?

19

quilt

Qq

question mark

quarters

queen

rhinoceros

ribbon

robot

rings

ruler

rooster

Rr

rock

One quarter alone is worth quite a lot.
If you save, save and save you could buy a robot,

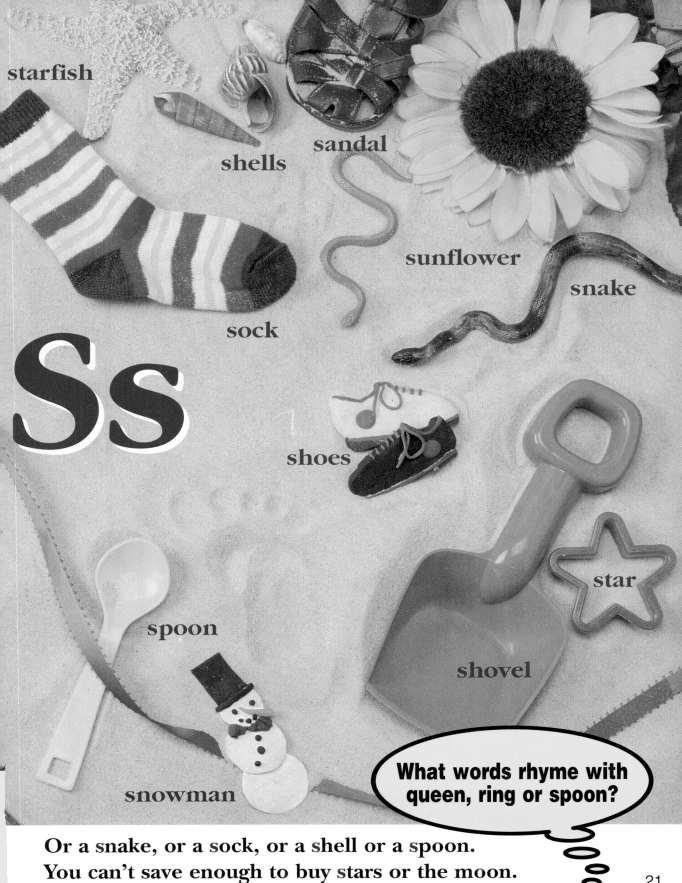

starfish

shells

sandal

sunflower

snake

sock

Ss

shoes

star

spoon

shovel

snowman

What words rhyme with queen, ring or spoon?

Or a snake, or a sock, or a shell or a spoon.
You can't save enough to buy stars or the moon.

21

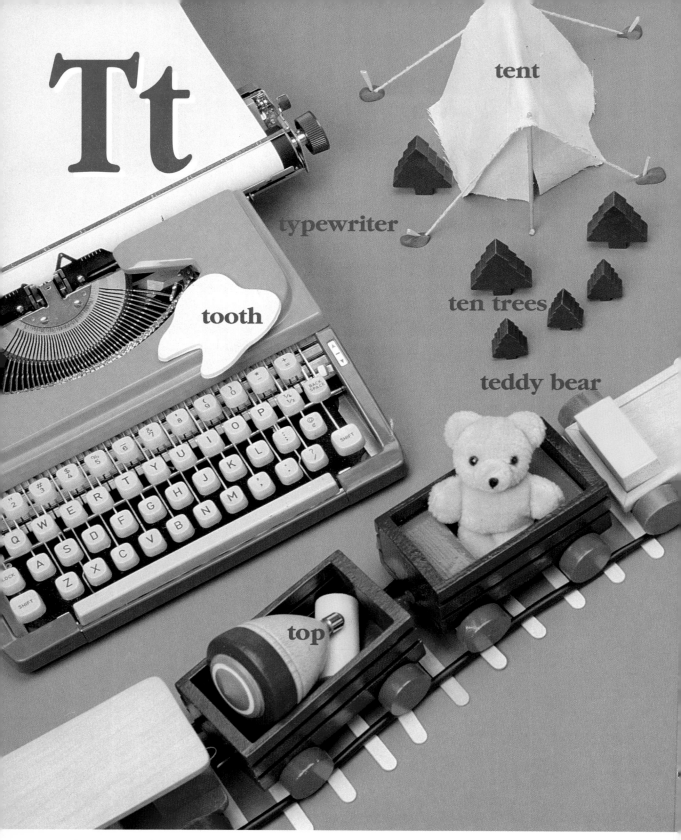

Tt

tent

typewriter

tooth

ten trees

teddy bear

top

On a train trip across the whole U.S.A.
Invite ten friends along. Start packing today!

Take your **teddy**, **umbrella** and **toothbrush, too.**
But leave your pet **turtle** home. He'll have nothing to do.

Vv

violin

BE MY ♥ VALENTINE

walnuts

vowels

watch

wagon

wheels

writing

Writing is fun!
Words are

words

Have a whale of an idea? Write it down and you'll see
Words do wonderful things. Watch and you'll agree.

24

Ww

window

world

whistle

water

whale

wolf

walrus

vegetables

worms

Try writing a sentence
with 3 **W** words,
or 4, or more!

Words can make a story about a wolf that can ski,
Or a valentine message that makes people happy.

Xx fox

box

yo-yo

yarn

zipper

Yy

hexagon

six

There are some things you don't want to keep in a box,
Like a wild zebra or a clever red fox,

zebra

zig zag

yawn

yardstick

Zz

zero

xylophone

What words make you think of bedtime?

Or a hot new yo-yo that's ready to spin,
Or a yawn — once it starts, you just can't keep it in.

27

A B C D E
Z
Y
X

WHAT'S THE BIG IDEA? ABOUT THE ALPHABET

Now that you've read this big idea book,
Step up and take a closer look
At 26 letters, A to Z —
The wonderful alphabet family!

Pick a few letters,
Put them in a crowd,
Hear how they sound
When you say them out loud.

You can rhyme words, sign words
Whisper them lowly.
Mold words, shape words
And see them grow slowly.

W V U T S

F G H I J K L M

Make a sentence, make two
Into a story by you.
Let your ideas grow
With your alphabet friends —
Friends who'll stick by you until

THE
END

R Q P O N

GLOSSARY
OF WORDS ABOUT WORDS

alphabet – the 26 letters we use to make words

book – pages put together that have stories, poems or interesting facts you can read

consonant – letter sounds you make by putting your lips, teeth or tongue together; like B, N or S

glossary – pages at the end of a book that tell you what some words and ideas in the book mean

idea – something you think of

index – a list of words in order by letter at the end of a book that tells you where to find the word in the book

letter – what the alphabet is made of; letters help us to make words and to make the right sounds when we read out loud

library – a place where you can borrow books to read

read – to look at words and understand what they say

sentence – a group of words put together that make sense spell – to use the right letters to make words

story – words and sentences you use to tell about something that happened, something you made up, or something you learned about

table of contents – the part in the beginning of the book that tells you what's in the book and where you can find it

title – the name of a book

vowel – A, E, I, O, U and sometimes Y; letter sounds you can make without touching your lips, teeth or tongue together

word – a group of letters that you can read, that mean something

write – to choose and make words (with a pencil, pen or computer) that tell someone something — a story, a poem, a report, directions, and so on

ABOUT THE ALPHABET

Try writing a sentence that uses all the letters in the alphabet.

Think of a story that starts in an attic and ends in the zoo.

Try finding rhymes for these words: muffin, diamond, hippopotamus.

What's the longest word you can think of?

How fast can you say the alphabet backwards?

Make a poster showing all the letters of the alphabet as animals or people.

Write a song that would explain vowels to someone else.

Get together with two or three friends and try to make all the letters of the alphabet using your bodies.